The
Gobble-uns'll
Git You
Ef You Don't
Watch
Out!

The Gobble-uns'll Git You Ef You Don't Watch Out!

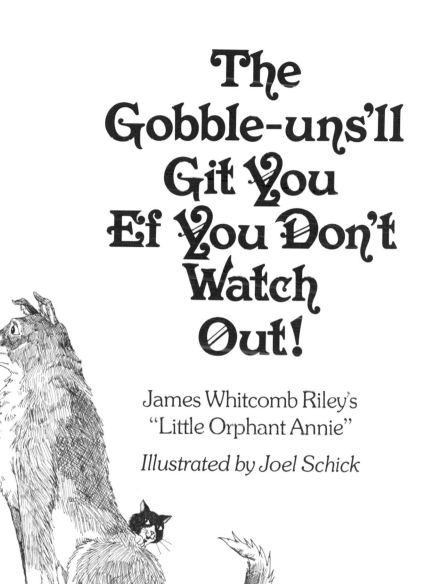

James Whitcomb Riley's
"Little Orphant Annie"

Illustrated by Joel Schick

J.B. Lippincott Company · Philadelphia and New York

Inscribed
with all faith and affection
to all the little children: the happy ones; and sad ones;
the sober and the silent ones; the boisterous and glad ones;
the good ones — Yes, the good ones too; and all the lovely bad ones.

J.W.R.

Illustrations and Illustrator's Note copyright © 1975 by Pongid Productions

All Rights Reserved

Printed in the United States of America

First Edition

U.S. Library of Congress Cataloging in Publication Data
Riley, James Whitcomb, 1849-1916.
The Gobble-uns'll git you ef you don't watch out!
SUMMARY: Gobble-un tales as told by little Orphant Annie.
[1. Behavior—Poetry. 2. American poetry] I. Schick, Joel, ill. II. Title.
PZ8.3.R47Go3   811'.4   74-23110   ISBN-0-397-31621-6

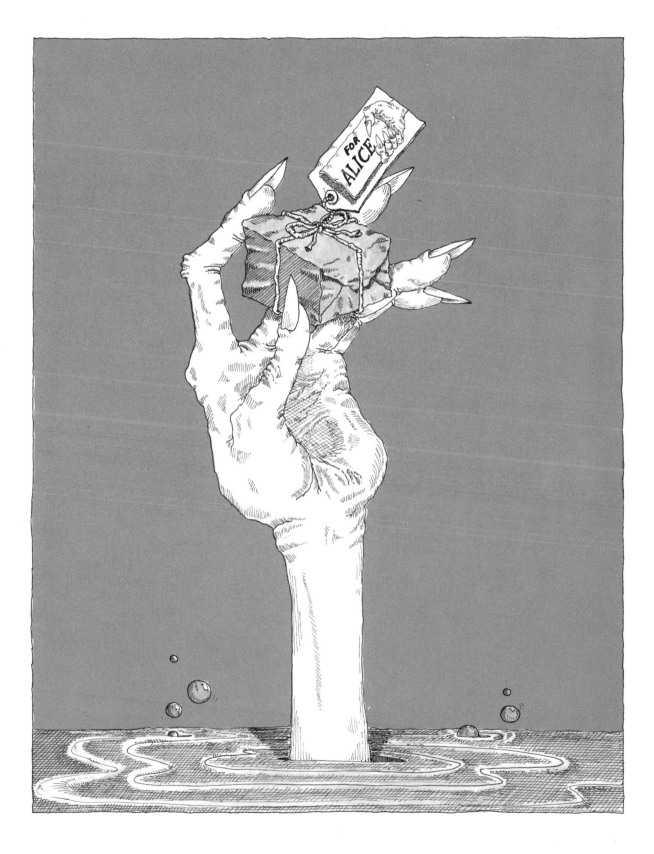

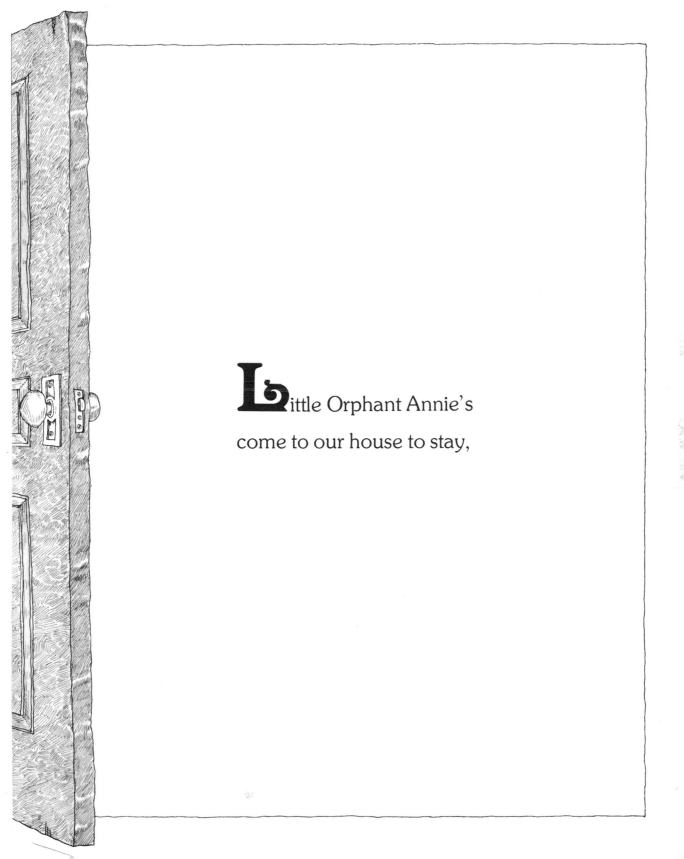

Little Orphant Annie's

come to our house to stay,

An' wash the cups an' saucers up,

an' brush the crumbs away,

An' shoo the chickens off the porch,

an' dust the hearth, an' sweep,

An' make the fire, an' bake the bread,

an' earn her board-an'-keep;

An' all us other childern,

when the supper things is done,

We set around the kitchen fire

an' has the mostest fun

A-list'nin' to the witch-tales

'at Annie tells about,

Onc't they was a little boy

wouldn't say his prayers—

So when he went to bed at night,
away up stairs,

His Mammy heerd him holler,

an' his Daddy heerd him bawl,

An' when they turn't the kivvers down,

HE WASN'T THERE AT ALL!

An' they seeked him in the rafter-room,
an' cubby-hole, an' press,
An' seeked him up the chimbly-flue,
an' ever'wheres, I guess;

But all they ever found was thist

his pants an' roundabout—

An' one time a little girl

'ud allus laugh an' grin,

An' make fun of ever' one,

an' all her blood an' kin;

An' onc't, when they was "company,"
an' old folks was there,
She mocked 'em an' shocked 'em,
an' said she didn't care!
An' thist as she kicked her heels,
an' turn't to run an' hide,

They was two great big Black Things
a-standin' by her side,

An' they snatched her through the ceilin'
'fore she knowed what she's about!

An' little Orphant Annie says,

when the blaze is blue,

An' the lamp-wick sputters,

an' the wind goes *woo-oo!*

An' you hear the crickets quit,

an' the moon is gray,

An' the lightnin'-bugs in dew

is all squenched away—

You better mind yer parents,

an' yer teachers fond an' dear,

An' churish them 'at loves you,

an' dry the orphant's tear,

An' he'p the pore an' needy ones

'at clusters all about,

ILLUSTRATOR'S NOTE

James Whitcomb Riley was born in 1849, in Greenfield, Indiana, where he spent much of his boyhood watching the local characters at the county courthouse. He left school at sixteen to travel around the state painting advertisements on barn walls, and later acting in a medicine show. By the time he settled down in Indianapolis to write, he really knew the people of his home state. He wrote about them and for them, in their own style. His poems were meant to be read out loud, and Riley himself used to read them for audiences. In fact, he was a popular entertainer in those days before movies and TV. Mark Twain once said that Riley's act was the funniest thing he had ever seen.

Riley wrote his poems in dialect, spelling words just the way Indiana people said them. He spelled "orphan" as *orphant* and "just" as *thist;* "if" became *ef,* and "cherish" came out *churish.* There are many more strange spellings which you'll find if you read this book again, especially if you read it out loud.

J.S.

ABOUT THE ILLUSTRATOR

Joel Schick and his wife, Alice, live in the western Massachusetts town of Monterey. Mr. Schick says, "My wife and I are both animal lovers. We have six cats, mostly former strays, and expect that someday we will look back on this time as the good old days when we had only six cats." Growing up in the midst of his father's Chicago print shop gave Mr. Schick an early interest in publishing. At age twelve he wrote and illustrated his own humor magazine, *Angry*, which he describes as "a complete disaster." He and his wife, a children's book author, currently head their own publishing service organization, Pongid Productions.